HEALING YOUR DYSFUNCTIONAL RELATIONSHIP

Transforming Pain into Growth: A Practical Guide to Healing Your Dysfunctional Relationship and Cultivating Lasting Connection

FRED K. FORTNER

TABLE OF CONTENT

Introduction: Navigating the Landscape of Healing in Your Relationships

Welcome to the journey of a lifetime—welcome to "Healing Your Dysfunctional Relationship." This book is not merely a guide; it is an immersive experience, a compass that navigates the intricate terrain of repairing and revitalizing relationships that may have been marred by dysfunction. As you embark on this odyssey, consider it a profound exploration into the heart of your connections, a journey that transcends the ordinary to unveil the extraordinary potential for healing and transformation.

The Tapestry of Relationships
At the core of our existence lies the tapestry of relationships—threads woven with shared laughter, intertwined emotions, and the delicate dance of connection. Yet, within the tapestry, there are knots, frays, and tangles

that can obscure the beauty of these relationships. This book is an invitation to unravel those knots, smooth out the frays, and transform the tangles into a tapestry that tells a story of resilience, growth, and enduring connection.

The Essence of Self-Discovery
Before we embark on the expedition of healing your relationship, we pause to delve into the profound realm of self-discovery. This chapter invites you to reflect on your own journey—your dreams, fears, and the intricate layers that form the essence of your being. Understanding yourself is the cornerstone of understanding your relationships, and it's a crucial first step on the path to healing.

Unmasking Dysfunction: A Candid Exploration
Dysfunction often wears a mask, concealing itself in the routines of daily life or the familiarity of patterns. In this section, we

strip away the mask, confronting dysfunction head-on. Through candid exploration and insightful revelations, we define dysfunction in its various forms—be it the silent erosion of communication, the weight of unresolved conflicts, or the echoes of unmet needs. The goal is to shed light on the shadows and empower you to recognize dysfunction within the intimate corners of your relationships.

Patterns That Bind: Breaking Free
Relationships are governed by patterns, some as delicate as a whispered secret and others as loud as an unspoken argument. This chapter unravels common patterns that may have bound your relationships in dysfunction. By understanding and challenging these patterns, you gain the freedom to break free from the chains that have constrained your connection, opening the door to a more harmonious dance of partnership.

The Echoes of Emotion: Understanding Impact

Beyond the visible surface of dysfunction lies a profound impact on the emotional and mental well-being of those involved. This section invites you to listen to the echoes of emotion—the silent reverberations that shape the landscape of your relationships. By understanding the depth of this impact, you lay the groundwork for a compassionate and holistic approach to healing.

The Call to Healing: Embracing the Journey Ahead

As we conclude this introduction, envision the chapters ahead not as mere pages but as stepping stones on the path to healing and growth. This book is a guide, offering not only insights and strategies but a heartfelt companion on your journey towards nurturing relationships that stand resilient in the face of adversity.

Embrace this process of transformation. Allow the words on these pages to be a mirror reflecting the potential for healing within you and your relationships. The subsequent chapters will guide you through practical techniques, thoughtful reflections, and actionable steps, all aimed at fostering profound and lasting change in the very fabric of your connections. The journey is yours, and the destination is a relationship that not only survives but thrives. Let the exploration begin.

Understanding Dysfunctional Relationships

In the intricate tapestry of human connection, relationships are the threads that weave the narrative of our lives. However, not all threads are smooth, and some may become entangled, leading to dysfunction. In this section, we embark on a comprehensive exploration, peeling back the layers to gain a profound understanding of dysfunctional relationships – what they are, how they manifest, and the profound impact they can have on our mental and emotional well-being.

1.1 Defining Dysfunction: Navigating the Complexity

The Multifaceted Nature of Dysfunction
Dysfunction in relationships is a nuanced concept that goes beyond mere disagreements. Here, we delve into the multifaceted nature of dysfunction, exploring its various forms—from breakdowns in communication and unresolved conflicts to power imbalances and emotional neglect. By defining dysfunction, we provide a framework for recognizing its presence within the intricate dynamics of your relationships.

The Interplay of Individual and Collective Dysfunction
Relationships are a dance between individuals, each bringing their own history,

fears, and aspirations to the partnership. This section examines the interplay of individual and collective dysfunction, highlighting how personal baggage can contribute to relational challenges. Understanding this interplay is crucial for unraveling the complexities that hinder the growth of healthy connections.

Dynamics of Control and Power in Dysfunction
Dysfunctional relationships often feature imbalances of control and power. Whether subtle or overt, these dynamics can poison the well of connection. We explore how control issues manifest, the impact they have on both partners, and strategies for regaining a sense of balance. By understanding power dynamics, you empower yourself to create relationships built on mutual respect and equality.

1.2 Recognizing Common Patterns: Illuminating the Shadows

The Invisible Scripts of Dysfunction

Patterns govern the behaviors and interactions within relationships, and dysfunctional ones can become like invisible scripts that dictate the narrative. This section sheds light on common patterns that contribute to dysfunction, such as avoidance, blame-shifting, or the repetition of unhealthy habits. Recognizing these patterns is the first step towards dismantling them and cultivating a more positive relational dynamic.

Breaking the Cycle: Challenging Repetitive Behaviors

Breaking free from the cycle of dysfunction requires a conscious effort to challenge and change repetitive behaviors. We delve into the intricacies of breaking the cycle, offering practical insights into recognizing, interrupting, and transforming detrimental patterns. By understanding the mechanisms at play, you gain the tools needed to foster healthier, more constructive interactions.

1.3 The Impact on Mental and Emotional Well-being: Unveiling the Silent Toll

Emotional Toll of Dysfunction

Dysfunctional relationships can exact a silent toll on mental and emotional well-being. This section explores the emotional landscape affected by dysfunction, unraveling the complexities of stress, anxiety, and even deeper emotional wounds. By acknowledging the emotional toll, you gain a heightened awareness of the urgency to instigate positive change in your relationship landscape.

The Ripple Effect on Mental Health

The impact of dysfunction extends far beyond the immediate participants, affecting the mental health of individuals and, by extension, the broader community. We examine the ripple effect of dysfunctional relationships, emphasizing the importance of addressing these issues not only for personal well-being but for the collective mental health of those involved.

In this in-depth exploration, we lay the groundwork for your journey towards healing and transformation. By understanding the multifaceted nature of dysfunction, recognizing common patterns, and acknowledging the profound impact on mental and emotional well-being, you've taken the first steps toward fostering positive change in your relationships. The subsequent chapters will guide you through practical strategies, empowering you to navigate the challenges and ultimately build relationships that thrive on connection, understanding, and mutual growth.

Part I: Self-Exploration and Awareness

Chapter 2: Reflecting on Your Relationship History

Welcome to the heart of self-discovery and transformation—Chapter 2: Reflecting on Your Relationship History. This chapter is a profound exploration into the layers of your past, designed to guide you through an in-depth examination of your experiences, the patterns woven through your relationships, and the emotional triggers that shape your interactions.

2.1 Examining Past Experiences: Tracing the Roots of Your Relationship Narrative

Unraveling Early Influences
Begin this journey by immersing yourself in the rich tapestry of your early experiences. Reflect on your childhood relationships, family dynamics, and significant events that have left an indelible mark on your

relational identity. By unraveling the threads of your early influences, you gain insights into the roots of your relationship narrative, understanding how the past has shaped your present perceptions and expectations.

Impact of Childhood Experiences on Adult Relationships
Childhood experiences form the bedrock of adult relationships. Delve into the impact of your formative years on the way you engage in connections today. Uncover the positive aspects that contribute to your strengths, as well as the challenges that may be rooted in early experiences. This introspection sets the stage for cultivating a deeper understanding of the intricacies within your current relationships.

2.2 Identifying Patterns in Your Relationships: The Dance of Recurring Themes

Recognizing Recurring Themes

Relationships often follow a familiar dance, with recurring themes and behaviors shaping the narrative. Engage in a meticulous examination of your relationships to identify these recurring patterns. Explore the dynamics of past connections, pinpointing common themes that may include communication styles, conflict resolution approaches, and relational roles. Recognizing these patterns is a crucial step toward breaking free from cycles that contribute to dysfunction.

Unveiling Communication Patterns

Communication serves as the lifeline of relationships. In this section, delve into the nuances of your communication patterns. Examine how you express emotions, navigate conflicts, and share vulnerabilities. Identify both healthy and problematic communication styles, gaining a comprehensive understanding of how your words and actions impact the dynamics of your relationships. This exploration lays the foundation for fostering more effective and enriching communication in the future.

2.3 Uncovering Personal Triggers: Navigating Emotional Terrain

Identifying Emotional Landmines
Emotions are intricately connected to past wounds, and personal triggers can act as emotional landmines within relationships. Take a courageous journey into the emotional terrain of your past. Identify specific events or circumstances that trigger strong emotional reactions. By understanding these emotional landmines, you empower yourself to navigate relationships with greater emotional intelligence and resilience.

The Intersection of Triggers and Dysfunctional Dynamics

Emotional triggers often intersect with dysfunctional relationship dynamics. In this section, explore the complex interplay between personal triggers and patterns of dysfunction. Understand how emotional sensitivities contribute to cycles of conflict or withdrawal. By untangling this intersection, you gain valuable insights into breaking free from detrimental patterns, fostering emotional growth, and creating healthier relational dynamics.

As you engage deeply with Chapter 2, envision it as a voyage into the very core of your being—the exploration of your relationship history, the identification of recurring patterns, and the illumination of personal triggers. Each revelation is a stepping stone toward healing and transformation, setting the stage for the practical strategies and actionable insights that will follow in the subsequent chapters.

Embrace the richness of this reflective journey as you pave the way for a more conscious, connected, and resilient approach to your relationships.

Chapter 3: Self-Discovery and Personal Growth

Welcome to the transformative exploration of Chapter 3: Self-Discovery and Personal Growth. This chapter serves as a crucial turning point in your journey, focusing on the cultivation of self-awareness, the nurturing of self-compassion, and the intentional setting of personal growth goals. Embrace this chapter as an opportunity for profound introspection, self-acceptance, and the initiation of a deliberate path toward personal development.

3.1 Embracing Self-Awareness: Illuminating the Inner Landscape

The Mirror of Reflection

Self-awareness is the cornerstone of personal growth. Begin by gazing into the mirror of reflection, examining your thoughts, emotions, and behaviors. Engage in a candid exploration of your strengths, weaknesses, values, and beliefs. By embracing self-awareness, you lay the foundation for understanding how you show up in relationships and the impact you have on those around you.

Unveiling Patterns Through Mindful Observation

Mindful observation is a powerful tool in the pursuit of self-awareness. Delve into the practice of observing your thoughts and reactions without judgment. Identify patterns that emerge in different situations, especially those replicated in your relationships. This mindful scrutiny allows you to uncover deeply ingrained behaviors and offers insights into areas for personal growth.

3.2 Cultivating Self-Compassion: Nurturing the Inner Sanctuary

Embracing Imperfection and Vulnerability

Self-compassion is the balm that heals the wounds of self-judgment. Explore the art of embracing imperfection and vulnerability. Acknowledge that, like everyone else, you are a work in progress. By fostering self-compassion, you create an inner sanctuary where mistakes are opportunities for learning, and vulnerabilities are embraced as part of the shared human experience.

Practicing Kindness Toward Yourself
Kindness is a powerful catalyst for personal growth. Learn to extend the same compassion to yourself that you would to a dear friend. Challenge your inner critic and replace self-critical thoughts with affirmations and encouragement. As you cultivate self-compassion, you build a resilient foundation that supports you through the challenges of self-discovery and transformation.

3.3 Setting Personal Growth Goals: Mapping the Journey Ahead

Defining Clear and Attainable Objectives
Personal growth thrives on purposeful direction. Begin by defining clear and

attainable personal growth objectives. Reflect on the areas identified through self-awareness where improvement or development is desired. Whether it's enhancing communication skills, managing stress more effectively, or fostering emotional intelligence, articulate goals that align with your aspirations.

Breaking Down Goals into Actionable Steps
The journey of personal growth becomes more manageable when goals are broken down into actionable steps. Develop a roadmap that outlines the specific actions you will take to achieve your objectives. These steps serve as guideposts along your path, ensuring that personal growth remains a dynamic and achievable process.

As you engage with the rich content of Chapter 3, envision it as a transformative workshop—an opportunity for self-discovery, self-compassion, and the intentional setting of personal growth goals.

Each section provides a toolkit for building a deeper understanding of yourself, cultivating resilience and kindness, and charting a course toward meaningful personal development. The insights gained in this chapter will serve as a compass for the chapters to come, guiding you through the practical strategies and transformative practices that will contribute to healing and growth in your relationships. Embrace the journey ahead as you invest in your own evolution and well-being.

Part II: Communication and Conflict Resolution

Chapter 4: Effective Communication Strategies

Welcome to Chapter 4, where we delve into the art of fostering meaningful connections through Effective Communication Strategies. This chapter acts as a practical guide, offering insights into active listening techniques, strategies for expressing yourself clearly and assertively, and navigating the intricate terrain of misunderstandings. Communication is the heartbeat of relationships, and mastering these skills will empower you to build stronger, more authentic connections.

4.1 Active Listening Techniques: Cultivating the Art of Presence

The Power of Undivided Attention
Active listening is the foundation of effective communication. Explore the transformative

power of undivided attention, where you fully immerse yourself in the speaker's words. Learn to set aside distractions, tune into verbal and non-verbal cues, and demonstrate genuine interest. This section equips you with the tools to cultivate presence, fostering a deeper connection with your communication partner.

Reflective Responses: Mirroring Understanding
Go beyond hearing words; delve into the realm of reflective responses. Understand the nuances of mirroring understanding through paraphrasing and summarizing. This technique not only confirms your comprehension but also conveys empathy and validates the speaker's perspective. Mastering reflective responses enhances the quality of your interactions, creating a more harmonious and supportive communication environment.

4.2 Expressing Yourself Clearly and Assertively: Honoring Your Voice

Clarity in Communication: Crafting Articulate Messages

Effective communication is a two-way street, requiring not only attentive listening but also clear and articulate expression. Explore the art of crafting messages with precision and clarity. Understand the impact of your words, tone, and body language. This section provides practical techniques for ensuring your messages are conveyed authentically and are open to mutual understanding.

The Assertive Edge: Balancing Expression and Respect

Assertiveness is the cornerstone of self-expression within relationships. Discover the delicate balance between expressing your needs, feelings, and opinions while respecting the perspectives of others. This section empowers you with assertive communication techniques, allowing you to navigate conversations with confidence, authenticity, and a commitment to mutual understanding.

4.3 Navigating Misunderstandings: Bridging Communication Gaps

Identifying Common Pitfalls in Communication

Misunderstandings are inevitable, but navigating them skillfully is an essential aspect of effective communication. Explore the common pitfalls that contribute to miscommunication, such as assumptions, unclear expressions, and differing interpretations. Recognizing these challenges lays the groundwork for proactive communication strategies to prevent and address misunderstandings.

Conflict Resolution Strategies: Transforming Challenges into Growth

Conflict, when approached constructively, can be a catalyst for growth. This section guides you through conflict resolution strategies, emphasizing the importance of active listening, assertiveness, and empathy. Learn to de-escalate tensions, find common ground, and transform misunderstandings into opportunities for deeper connection and mutual understanding.

As you immerse yourself in the content of Chapter 4, envision it as a communication workshop—a space where you refine your ability to listen actively, express yourself assertively, and skillfully navigate the intricacies of misunderstandings. The tools and techniques provided in this chapter are the building blocks for fostering healthier and more meaningful connections in your relationships. Embrace the transformative power of effective communication, for within it lies the key to nurturing thriving connections.

Chapter 5: Conflict Resolution and Healthy Disagreements

Conflict is an inevitable part of human interactions, but it's how we navigate and resolve it that defines the health of our relationships. In this chapter, we explore the nature of conflict, introduce constructive resolution techniques, and delve into the art of building compromise to find common ground.

5.1 Understanding the Nature of Conflict: Decoding the Language of Disagreement

Embracing Conflict as a Catalyst for Growth

Conflict is not inherently negative; rather, it's a dynamic force that can lead to growth and deeper understanding. Explore the positive potential of conflict, understanding it as a catalyst for change, innovation, and strengthened connections. This section challenges common misconceptions about conflict, encouraging you to view it as an opportunity for transformation.

Identifying Root Causes: Peeling Back the Layers of Discontent

To resolve conflict effectively, one must address its root causes. Engage in a deep exploration to identify the underlying issues contributing to disagreements. Whether rooted in miscommunication, unmet needs, or differing values, understanding the core of the conflict is the first step toward constructive resolution.

5.2 Constructive Conflict Resolution Techniques: Mastering the Art of Resolution

Active Listening in Conflict: The Healing Power of Understanding

Active listening extends beyond everyday conversations into the realm of conflict resolution. Discover how the healing power of understanding through active listening can de-escalate tensions, validate emotions, and pave the way for constructive dialogue. This section equips you with specific techniques to apply active listening effectively during conflict.

Assertiveness in Conflict: Expressing Needs Respectfully

Assertiveness is a key component of navigating conflict. Learn how to express your needs, feelings, and opinions assertively, promoting transparency and authenticity. This section provides practical tools for balancing assertiveness with respect, creating a dialogue that fosters understanding and collaboration.

5.3 Building Compromise and Finding Common Ground: The Art of Collaboration

The Dance of Compromise: Balancing Give and Take

Compromise is the heartbeat of conflict resolution, requiring a delicate dance of give and take. Explore the art of finding middle ground and making concessions without sacrificing core values. This section provides strategies for building compromise that nurtures mutual understanding and creates win-win solutions.

Seeking Common Ground: Bridging Differences for Connection
Finding common ground is the bridge that spans differences, fostering connection and unity. Discover techniques for seeking commonality, emphasizing shared values, goals, and aspirations. This section guides you through the process of transcending differences and building a foundation for collaboration and harmonious relationships.

Envision the content of this chapter as as a roadmap for transforming conflicts into opportunities for growth and connection. The techniques and insights provided here are not only tools for resolving disagreements but pathways toward building stronger, more resilient relationships. Embrace the challenges of conflict with the knowledge that, when navigated skillfully, it can lead to deeper

understanding and the fortification of the
bonds you share.

Part III: Rebuilding Connection

Chapter 6: Rebuilding Trust and Intimacy

Welcome to the heart of transformation—Chapter 6, where we embark on the profound journey of Rebuilding Trust and Intimacy. In the aftermath of challenges and conflicts, the path to healing requires a deliberate focus on restoring the pillars of trust and intimacy within your relationships. This chapter serves as a guide, offering insights, strategies, and practices to help you navigate this intricate terrain and foster connections that are not only resilient but also deeply meaningful.

Navigating the Landscape of Trust and Intimacy
Trust and intimacy are the pillars upon which healthy relationships stand tall. In the

face of adversity or the aftermath of conflicts, these pillars may waver, requiring intentional effort to rebuild. Understanding the profound impact of trust and intimacy on the dynamics of connection is the first step toward navigating the landscape of rebuilding.

6.1 Understanding the Role of Trust in Relationships

Trust as the Glue of Connection
Trust serves as the invisible glue that binds relationships together. This section explores the multifaceted role of trust, delving into its influence on communication, emotional safety, and the overall well-being of connections. By understanding the centrality of trust, you lay the groundwork for rebuilding and reinforcing the foundations of your relationships.

The Impact of Broken Trust
When trust is broken, its repercussions echo through the emotional landscape. Delve into

the profound consequences of fractured trust, recognizing the emotional toll it takes on individuals and the relational fabric. Acknowledging the depth of this impact becomes a crucial starting point for the healing journey.

6.2 Strategies for Rebuilding Trust

Transparency and Open Communication: Rebuilding Bridges

Transparency and open communication form the bedrock of trust restoration. This section provides practical strategies for fostering transparent, honest, and open conversations. By addressing the events that led to the breach of trust, you create pathways for rebuilding bridges and initiating the healing process.

Consistency and Reliability: Building Trustworthiness

Consistency and reliability are the building blocks of trustworthiness. Explore actionable strategies for cultivating trust through consistent actions, reliability in commitments, and follow-through. This section guides you in establishing a trustworthy foundation that contributes to the gradual restoration of trust.

Establishing Boundaries and Accountability: Safeguarding Trust
Trust is safeguarded through clear boundaries and accountability. Delve into the process of establishing healthy boundaries and accountability measures that create a secure environment within the relationship. As you navigate this section, you'll discover practical ways to rebuild trust by fostering a sense of safety and respect.

6.3 Rediscovering Intimacy

Emotional Intimacy: Cultivating a Deeper Connection
Emotional intimacy forms the essence of profound connections. This section explores strategies for cultivating emotional intimacy, emphasizing vulnerability, active

listening, and empathetic understanding. By creating an environment where emotions are shared authentically, you pave the way for a deeper and more meaningful connection.

Physical Intimacy: Reconnecting Through Touch and Presence
Physical intimacy is a language that transcends words, rekindling the flame of connection. Rediscover the nuances of physical intimacy, emphasizing the importance of touch, presence, and shared moments. This section provides insights into rebuilding physical intimacy as a means of strengthening the bond between partners.

The strategies and insights offered here are not mere tools; they are pathways toward fostering a renewed sense of trust and intimacy. Embrace this chapter as an opportunity for transformation, recognizing that the intentional rebuilding of trust and intimacy can lead to relationships that are not only resilient but also enriched with a depth of understanding and closeness.

Rebuilding trust and intimacy is a delicate process, requiring intention, patience, and a commitment to vulnerability. In this chapter, we navigate the intricacies of trust, provide practical strategies for rebuilding it, and explore the nuances of rediscovering intimacy to foster stronger, more resilient connections.

Chapter 7: Cultivating Emotional Connection

Welcome to Chapter 7, a profound exploration into the art of Cultivating Emotional Connection within your relationships. This chapter serves as a guide to fostering emotional intimacy, enhancing empathy, and embracing the transformative power of vulnerability. As you navigate this chapter, envision it as a sanctuary for deepening the emotional bonds that form the heart and soul of meaningful connections.

7.1 Fostering Emotional Intimacy: The Heartbeat of Connection

Embracing Emotional Intimacy as a Pillar of Connection

Emotional intimacy is the lifeblood of profound connections. In this section, we explore the foundational role of emotional intimacy, recognizing it as a pillar that sustains and nourishes relationships. By understanding the depth and significance of emotional intimacy, you pave the way for intentional practices that foster a more profound connection with your partner.

Practices for Fostering Emotional Intimacy
Delve into practical practices for cultivating emotional intimacy. From mindful communication to shared experiences, this section offers actionable strategies to create an emotional space where both partners feel seen, heard, and understood. By incorporating these practices into your relationship, you lay the groundwork for a richer and more meaningful connection.

7.2 Enhancing Empathy in Your Relationship: The Bridge of Understanding

The Essence of Empathy in Connection
Empathy serves as the bridge that connects hearts and minds in relationships. This section explores the essence of empathy, emphasizing its role in deepening understanding and fostering emotional connection. By honing the skills of

empathetic listening and perspective-taking, you enhance the emotional intelligence within your relationship.

Practical Strategies for Cultivating Empathy
Empathy is a skill that can be cultivated and strengthened. Discover practical strategies for enhancing empathy in your relationship, including active listening, validating emotions, and practicing non-judgmental understanding. As you integrate these strategies into your interactions, you create a compassionate and empathetic foundation for a more connected partnership.

7.3 The Power of Vulnerability: Opening the Door to Authentic Connection

Understanding Vulnerability as a Strength
Vulnerability is not a weakness but a profound strength that opens the door to authentic connection. This section explores the transformative power of vulnerability in relationships, encouraging you to embrace

your authentic selves and share your true feelings with your partner. By understanding vulnerability as a courageous act, you create space for genuine and deep connection.

Navigating the Challenges of Vulnerability
While vulnerability is powerful, it can also be challenging. This section provides insights into navigating the fears and insecurities that may arise when opening up to your partner. By addressing these challenges with compassion and understanding, you create an environment where both partners feel safe to be vulnerable, fostering a deeper level of intimacy.

As you engage with the content of Chapter 7, see it as a transformative journey into the heart of emotional connection. The practices, strategies, and insights provided here are not just tools; they are pathways toward creating a relationship infused with emotional richness, empathy, and vulnerability. Embrace this chapter as an opportunity for profound connection, recognizing that the intentional cultivation of emotional bonds can lead to relationships that are not only enduring but also deeply fulfilling.

Part IV: Overcoming Challenges Together

Welcome to Part IV, where we confront the external challenges that life presents within the context of your relationship. In Chapter 8, we delve into Navigating External Challenges as a united front. This chapter serves as a guide to overcoming financial struggles, balancing work and personal life, and navigating the complexities of family dynamics and interference. As you navigate this chapter, envision it as a roadmap for fortifying your relationship against external pressures and emerging stronger together.

Chapter 8: Navigating External Challenges

External challenges can test the resilience of any relationship. In this chapter, we explore strategies and insights to navigate financial struggles, strike a balance between work and personal life, and manage the dynamics of family interference. Together, let's build a foundation that empowers you and your partner to overcome external challenges and emerge even more connected.

8.1 Financial Struggles: Weathering the Storms Together

Understanding the Impact of Financial Struggles on Relationships

Financial struggles can exert significant pressure on relationships. This section explores the emotional and relational impact of financial challenges, shedding light on the common stressors that couples face. By understanding the dynamics at play, you'll be better equipped to navigate these challenges as a team.

Strategies for Overcoming Financial Struggles

Delve into practical strategies for weathering financial storms together. From effective communication about money to budgeting and financial planning, this section provides actionable insights to help you and your partner align your financial goals, navigate challenges, and build a secure financial foundation for your relationship.

8.2 Balancing Work and Personal Life: Creating Harmony in Partnership

Recognizing the Impact of Work-Life Balance on Relationships
Balancing the demands of work and personal life is a common challenge in today's fast-paced world. Explore the impact of work-life balance on relationships, recognizing the importance of creating harmony between professional and personal responsibilities. This section provides insights into common pitfalls and challenges associated with work-life balance.

Strategies for Achieving Work-Life Balance as a Couple
Achieving work-life balance is a shared endeavor. Discover practical strategies for maintaining equilibrium, including effective

communication about priorities, setting boundaries, and prioritizing quality time together. By implementing these strategies, you and your partner can create a harmonious partnership that supports both personal and professional fulfillment.

8.3 Family Dynamics and Interference: Navigating Complexities Together

Understanding the Impact of Family Dynamics on Relationships
Family dynamics and interference can pose unique challenges to relationships. This section explores the impact of extended family on your partnership, acknowledging the complexities that may arise. Understanding the dynamics at play allows you to approach these challenges with empathy and a united front.

Strategies for Managing Family Dynamics and Interference
Navigate the complexities of family dynamics and interference with grace and

resilience. From setting boundaries to fostering open communication with extended family members, this section provides practical strategies to strengthen your relationship against external pressures. By aligning your responses and expectations, you and your partner can create a united front in managing family dynamics.

As you engage with the content of Chapter 8, envision it as a toolkit for navigating external challenges hand-in-hand with your partner. The strategies and insights provided here are not just solutions; they are pathways toward building a resilient relationship that can withstand the tests of external pressures. Embrace this chapter as an opportunity for growth and unity, recognizing that overcoming challenges together can deepen your connection and fortify the bond you share.

Chapter 9: Maintaining Progress and Preventing Relapse

Welcome to Chapter 9, a pivotal exploration into sustaining the progress you've made in your relationship journey. This chapter serves as a guide to creating relationship maintenance strategies, recognizing warning signs of regression, and seeking professional support when needed. As you engage with this chapter, envision it as a compass for maintaining the health and vibrancy of your relationship, ensuring that the strides you've taken continue to propel you forward.

9.1 Creating Relationship Maintenance Strategies: Nurturing the Seeds of Progress

Understanding the Importance of Relationship Maintenance
Relationships, like gardens, require ongoing care to thrive. This section explores the significance of relationship maintenance, emphasizing that sustaining progress is as vital as making it. By understanding the

value of consistent effort, you'll be motivated to create strategies that nurture the seeds of progress you've planted in your relationship.

Practical Strategies for Relationship Maintenance

Delve into practical strategies for maintaining the health and vibrancy of your relationship. From regular check-ins and quality time to shared goals and ongoing communication, this section provides a toolkit for cultivating a relationship that continues to evolve and deepen. Implementing these strategies will fortify the foundation you've built and support ongoing growth.

9.2 Recognizing Warning Signs of Regression: A Vigilant Partnership

Identifying Common Warning Signs

Even in the healthiest relationships, warning signs of regression may appear. This section guides you in recognizing common indicators, such as communication breakdowns, emotional distance, or recurring conflicts. Understanding these warning signs empowers you to address challenges proactively, preventing regression before it takes hold.

Strategies for Addressing Regression
Should warning signs manifest, having strategies to address regression is crucial. Explore proactive approaches for addressing challenges, including open communication, revisiting shared goals, and seeking mutual understanding. By incorporating these strategies into your relationship toolkit, you and your partner can collaboratively navigate difficult periods and steer the relationship back on course.

9.3 Seeking Professional Support When Needed: Strengthening the Support Network

Normalizing the Need for Professional Support

Recognizing when to seek professional support is a sign of strength, not weakness. This section destigmatizes the notion of seeking help, emphasizing that professional guidance can be a valuable resource in maintaining a healthy relationship. Normalizing this step opens the door for couples to proactively engage with professionals when needed.

Types of Professional Support and When to Seek It

Explore the types of professional support available, from couples counseling to individual therapy. Understand when seeking professional guidance is warranted, such as during times of prolonged conflict, significant life transitions, or persistent challenges. This section provides a roadmap for navigating the decision to seek professional support and guides you in finding the right resources for your unique relationship needs.

As you immerse yourself in the content of Chapter 9, envision it as a compass guiding you through the ongoing journey of relationship growth. The strategies and insights provided here are not just tools; they are pathways toward creating a relationship that continues to thrive and evolve. Embrace this chapter as an opportunity for proactive investment in the well-being of your partnership, ensuring that the progress you've made becomes a foundation for a resilient and flourishing relationship.

Conclusion: Celebrating Growth and Lasting Transformation

Congratulations on reaching the conclusion of this transformative journey in "Healing Your Dysfunctional Relationship." As we wrap up this guide, let's celebrate the achievements you've made, recognize the ongoing nature of the relationship healing journey, and embrace the continuous growth that lies ahead.

10.1 Acknowledging Achievements: Milestones on the Path to Healing

Reflecting on Personal and Relationship Growth

Take a moment to reflect on the growth you and your partner have experienced throughout this journey. Acknowledge the milestones—both big and small—that mark your progress. Celebrate the positive changes in communication, understanding, and connection. This section serves as a space for recognizing the efforts and resilience that have led to tangible improvements in your relationship.

Cultivating Gratitude for the Healing Process
Gratitude is a powerful emotion that enhances well-being and connection. Cultivate gratitude for the healing process you've undertaken together. Acknowledge the challenges you've faced and express appreciation for the strength, commitment, and mutual support that have sustained you. By recognizing and celebrating achievements, you reinforce the positive momentum for lasting transformation.

10.2 Embracing the Continuous Journey of Relationship Healing: A Dynamic Evolution

Understanding that Growth Is Ongoing
Healing and growth within a relationship are continuous processes. Recognize that the journey doesn't end here—it evolves. This section encourages you to embrace the idea that relationships are dynamic and

require ongoing attention and effort. Understand that growth is a lifelong commitment, and each stage of the journey brings new opportunities for connection and understanding.

Cultivating a Mindset of Continuous Improvement

As you move forward, adopt a mindset of continuous improvement. View challenges as opportunities for learning and growth. This section provides insights into cultivating a proactive approach to relationship dynamics, fostering an environment where both partners are committed to evolving individually and as a couple. Embrace the notion that the journey itself is a source of richness and depth.

In Conclusion: A Celebration of Healing and Growth

In closing, "Healing Your Dysfunctional Relationship" has been more than a guide—it has been a companion on your journey toward a healthier, more fulfilling connection. Celebrate the progress you've made, the insights you've gained, and the foundation you've built for lasting transformation. Remember that the continuous journey of relationship healing is a testament to your commitment, resilience, and love.

May your relationship be a source of joy, connection, and mutual support. As you step into the future, carry the lessons learned and the growth experienced with you. The pages of this guide are a resource to revisit whenever needed, a reminder of the strength inherent in your relationship and the potential for ever-deepening connection.

Thank you for allowing "Healing Your Dysfunctional Relationship" to be a part of your journey. May your path ahead be filled with continued growth, understanding, and

the enduring power of a thriving and
resilient relationship.

www.ingramcontent.com/pod-product-compliance
Lightning Source LLC
Chambersburg PA
CBHW070806250726
48662CB00004B/2001